For Juniper Wren Thomas, a lover of all animals

STERLING CHILDREN'S BOOKS
New York

An Imprint of Sterling Publishing Co., Inc.
1166 Avenue of the Americas
New York, NY 10036

ISBN 978-1-4549-2991-8

Distributed in Canada by Sterling Publishing Co., Inc.
c/o Canadian Manda Group, 664 Annette Street
Toronto, Ontario M6S 2C8, Canada
Distributed in the United Kingdom by GMC Distribution Services
Castle Place, 166 High Street, Lewes, East Sussex BN7 1XU, England
Distributed in Australia by NewSouth Books
University of New South Wales, Sydney, NSW 2052, Australia

For information about custom editions, special sales, and premium and corporate purchases, please contact Sterling Special Sales at 800-805-5489 or specialsales@sterlingpublishing.com.

Manufactured in China

Lot #:
2   4   6   8   10   9   7   5   3   1
12/18

sterlingpublishing.com

PHOTOGRAPHS:
COVER Front: F1online digitale Bildagentur GmbH/Alamy; **Back:** Guenterguni/istock

INTERIOR: Alamy: Cgwp.co.uk 15, Valerii Kaliuzhnyi 25 (Malayan), Anette Mossbacher 21, Dmitriy Shironosov 6, Travel Images 25, (Indochinese), Avalon/Photoshot License (skin) 27, XinHua 10; **AnimalsAnimals:** © J & C Sohns (leopard) 11; **Ardea:** Chris Brunskill/Animals Animals/Earth Scenes 14; **Getty Images:** Beverly Joube 12, Svetlana Simeonova (kittens) 11; **iStock:** Anankkml 5, Anudarshan Photography 8, Appfind 13, Backiris (bengal) 24, GlobalP (sumantran) 24, Guenterguni 29, Zoran Kolundzija 16, Mari Art 24 (siberian), Mark Malkinson 20, RichVintage 11 (football players), Rinelle 7, Syafiq_3003 22; **Minden:** Anup Shah/NPL 9; **Shutterstock.com:** Artem Avetisyan 19, Sundari 23, Pyty 26, Thes2680 17, Popova Valeriya (south china) 25; **SuperStock:** © Illustrated London News Ltd/Pantheon (hunters) 27, © NaturePL 31, © Kevin Schafer/Minden Pictures 28, © Woodfall Wild Images/Photoshot 2—3

Just Ask!

DO TIGERS STAY UP LATE?

...and Other Tiger-ific Questions

MARY KAY CARSON

STERLING CHILDREN'S BOOKS
New York

Do tigers make good pets?

NO! Tigers, lions, leopards, and cougars are wild cats. But they are **relatives** of house cats. All cats belong to the same **feline** family. A house cat is like a tiny tame tiger that is safe to pet!

All cats are natural-born hunters. The body of a cat has many weapons: Teeth for chomping. Legs for pouncing. Claws for grabbing. Cats are expert **predators**.

Do tigers purr?

NOPE. Purring is not for big cats. Tigers growl and grunt. They also roar! Tigers roar to get attention.

"Come here, cubs!" says a tiger mother's roar.

"Leave my forest!" says a male tiger's roar.

A tiger's roar is super loud. It can be heard from far away. How far? The distance that an hour of walking can take you. That's far!

Can a tiger sleep on the sofa?

Tigers are the biggest cats on Earth. Some male tigers grow to be 12 feet (4 m) long! A sofa that size would fit two grown-ups sleeping head-to-toe.

If a tiger is trying to nap on your sofa, just let it.

Does a tiger weigh more than fifty kitty cats?

Most grown tigers weigh at least 300 pounds (136 kg). But a big 12-foot (4-m) tiger? It can weigh 700 pounds (318 kg). That's as heavy as three football players. It's the weight of four or five leopards, or about sixty house cats. That's a lot of fur!

Why do tigers have stripes?

A tiger in the zoo is an eye-catching creature. You'd know that orange fur with dark stripes anywhere.

But a tiger on the hunt is hard to see. Its up-and-down stripes **camouflage** it. The stripes blend in with stalks of grass and skinny trees.

Can you spot the tiger?

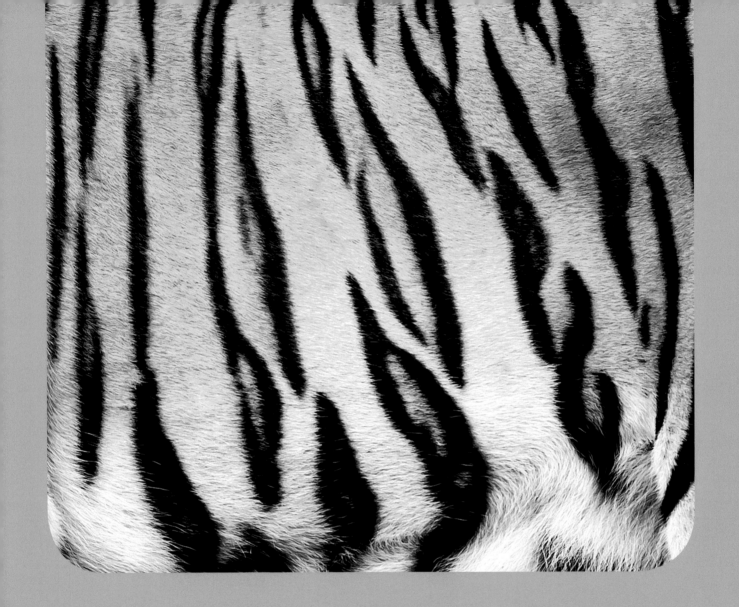

No two tigers have identical stripes. Each one has its own pattern, like a fingerprint. Tiger fur isn't the only thing that is striped. The skin underneath is, too!

Are tigers vegetarians?

No way! Tigers are meat-eating **carnivores**. They are strong predators that can kill **prey** larger than themselves. Deer, wild pigs, and water buffalo are on a tiger's menu.

A tiger stalks its future dinner. It waits, hidden from view. When the moment is right . . . the tiger pounces! Its claws dig in and hold on. Its big **canine** teeth sink into the prey's neck. Dinner time!

Do tigers stay up late?

Yes! Tigers are out and about at night. They are **nocturnal** predators. Nighttime is hunting time. Darkness helps hide a tiger from its prey.

After dark is also when tigers go on patrol. Adult tigers have huge **territories**, 20 square miles (32 square kilometers) on average. Tigers mark their territories with scratches and scents. They rub against trees, scratch up logs, and pee on rocks. These messages say: *My territory! Not yours!*

Would a tiger win a marathon?

NOPE. Tigers run fast, but not far. A running tiger gets tired quickly. It needs to surprise its prey to catch it. If a tiger misses on the first pounce, it usually gives up. A tiger can't run down an escaping antelope.

Sometimes a week goes by without a successful hunt. The stomach of a tiger growls, too. When a tiger makes a kill, it eats and eats. Once the tiger finishes, it finds water. After a long drink, this hunter naps.

Do tigers have kittens?

NOPE. Babies of big cats are called **cubs**, not kittens. Tiger moms have litters of two or three cubs. Tiger cubs are born with their eyes closed, just like kittens.

Do tigers get lonely?

Not really.
Tiger cubs live with their mom for about two years until they are grown up. Adults tigers live alone. If two tigers meet in the forest they might say hello. How? By rubbing heads.

Do tigers swim?

Yes! Tigers love the water. These big cats can swim for miles. What a splashy way to travel! Tigers will lay in water to cool off, too. *Ahhh.*

Do they sunbathe?

No. Tigers like shady, not sunny, spots to nap. Tigers are not cool cats. Those fur coats are hot! Tigers can overheat easily.

Are all tigers the same?

There are six kinds of tigers. Their names describe where they live.

Siberian tigers are the biggest. They can be twice as big as the Sumatrans, the smallest tigers.

BENGAL

SUMATRAN

SIBERIAN

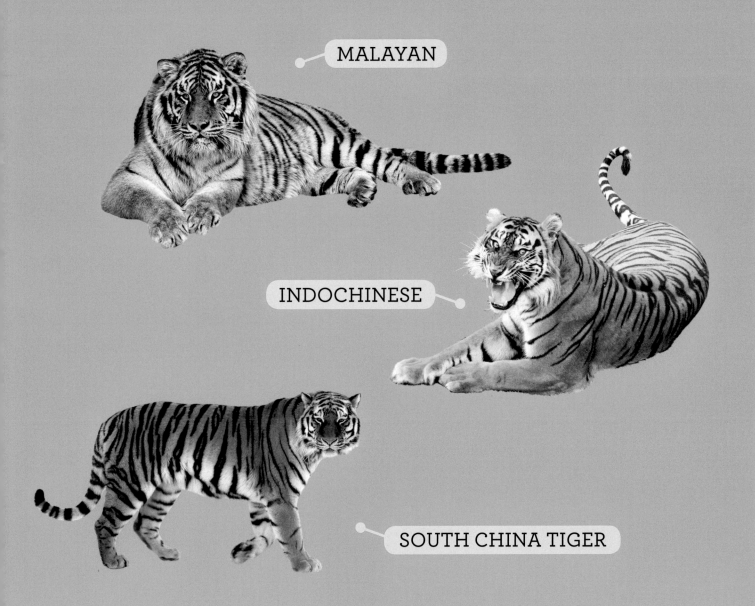

MALAYAN

INDOCHINESE

SOUTH CHINA TIGER

Do tigers live around here?

Wild tigers live only in Asia. India is home to more than half of the world's tigers. Tigers live in Indonesia and Malaysia, too.

Are tigers dangerous?

Yes! Tigers are big. They have sharp teeth and claws. That makes them dangerous.

Tigers usually stay away from humans. They avoid towns and farms. But people cause problems for tigers. Humans are why tigers are **endangered**. Tigers are in danger of going **extinct**. Fewer than 4,000 tigers roam the wild today.

Help the Tigers!

These groups are working to protect wild tigers.
Find out how:

• World Wildlife Fund: www.worldwildlife.org/species/tiger
• Panthera: www.panthera.org/initiative/save-tiger-fund
• Tiger Conservation Campaign: http://support.mnzoo.org/tigercampaign

Tiger Words to Know

camouflage – blending in with surroundings

canine – long, pointed tooth

carnivores – meat eaters

cubs – babies of meat-eating animals

endangered – in danger of dying off

extinct – no longer living

feline - cat

nocturnal – active at night

predators – animals that hunt to eat

prey – animal hunted for food

relatives – family members

territory – area an animal lives in and defends

Index